Italian Cooking Made Easy

This Italian Cookbook Will Become Your All-Time Favorite

BY: Allie Allen

COOK & ENJOY

Copyright 2019 Allie Allen

Copyright Notes

This book is written as an informational tool. While the author has taken every precaution to ensure the accuracy of the information provided therein, the reader is warned that they assume all risk when following the content. The author will not be held responsible for any damages that may occur as a result of the readers' actions.

The author does not give permission to reproduce this book in any form, including but not limited to: print, social media posts, electronic copies or photocopies, unless permission is expressly given in writing.

My Gift to You for Buying My Book!

I would like to extend an exclusive offer to receive free and discounted eBooks every day! This special gift is my way of saying thanks. If you fill in the subscription box below you will begin to receive special offers directly to your email.

Not only that! You will also receive notifications letting you know when an offer will expire. You will never miss a chance to get a free book! Who wouldn't want that?

Fill in the subscriber information below and get started today!

https://allie-allen.getresponsepages.com/

Table of Contents

Delicious Italian Cooking Recipes 6

1) Classic Shrimp Scampi.. 7

2) Easy Italian Lasagna 10

3) Homemade Italian Style Beef 14

4) Italian Style Stuffed Peppers... 16

5) Easy Salmon in Foil 19

6) Easy Italian Style Potato Salad... 23

7) Sweet Tasting Lemon Ricotta Cookies 25

8) Italian Style Sausage Tortellini Soup.............................. 29

9) Hearty Chicken Tetrazzini 33

10) Savory Mushroom Bocconcini Salad 38

11) Classic Chicken Parmesan 41

12) Classic Caprese and Pesto Salad................................... 46

13) Classic Cippino... 49

14) Slow Cooker Style Chicken Alfredo 52

15) Savory Alfredo Peppered Shrimp 55

16) Classic Bruschetta 59

17) Classic Zuppa Toscana 62

18) Margherita Style Pizza 65

19) Slow Cooker Style Eggplant Parmesan 69

20) Spaghetti Marinara 72

21) Easy Italian Style Penne and Pasta 75

22) Traditional Mushroom Risotto 78

23) Italian Style Meatloaf 81

24) Baked Spaghetti and Meatballs 84

25) Classic Italian Potato Salad 88

26) Italian Style Wine Biscuits 91

About the Author 94

Author's Afterthoughts 96

Delicious Italian Cooking Recipes

sssssssssssssssssssssssssssssssssssssssssssssss

1) Classic Shrimp Scampi

If you are a huge fan of shrimp, then you are going to love this Italian classic. This dish is incredibly delicious and will certainly leave you wanting more.

Yield: 2 Pounds of Shrimp Scampi

Cooking Time: 30 Minutes

List of Ingredients:

- 2 Pounds of Shrimp, Peeled, Deveined and Cut Butterfly Style
- 3 Tablespoons of Olive Oil
- 2 Tablespoons of White Wine, Dry Variety
- 12 Tablespoons of Butter, Unsalted and Softened
- 4 Cloves of Garlic, Minced
- ¼ Cup of Shallots, Minced
- 3 Tablespoons of Parsley, Fresh and Minced
- 1 teaspoon of Rosemary, Fresh and Minced
- ¼ teaspoons of Red Pepper Flakes
- 1 teaspoon of Lemon Zest, Freshly Grated
- 2 Tablespoons of Lemon Juice, Fresh
- 1 Egg, Yolk Only
- 2/3 Cup of Bread Flakes, Dried
- Some Lemon Wedges for Serving and Garnish
- Dash of Salt and Pepper for Taste

ssssssssssssssssssssssssssssssssssssssssssss

Procedure:

1. The first thing that you will want to do is preheat your oven to 425 degrees. While your oven is heating up place your first three ingredients into a medium sized mixing bowl. Season your shrimp with a dash of salt and pepper and toss thoroughly to coat. Allow the shrimp to sit in this mixture for a couple of minutes to fully marinate in the juices.

2. Next stir together your remaining ingredients into a medium sized bowl and season with some more salt and pepper for taste. Set this mixture aside.

3. Then place your shrimp inside of a gratin dish, making sure that the tails are pointing up and the cut side is facing down. Drizzle your prepared marinade over the shrimp and spread your garlic butter mixture over each piece of shrimp as well.

4. Place your shrimp into the oven to bake for at least 12 minutes. Then broil the shrimp for at least 1 to 2 minutes.

5. Remove from oven and serve right away with lemon wedges for garnish. Enjoy!

2) Easy Italian Lasagna

Who isn't a fan of Lasagna? Well, with this recipe now you can enjoy this dish whenever you wish. With this recipe this dish is easy to make and packed full of that authentic Italian taste.

Yield: 1 Whole Lasagna Dish

Cooking Time: 1 Hour and 20 Minutes

Ingredients for Your Pasta:

- 12 Sheets of Lasagna Noodles, Your Favorite Brand
- ¾ Pound of Mozzarella Cheese, Sliced
- ¾ Cup of Parmesan Cheese, Finely Grated

Ingredients for Your Meat Sauce:

- 2 Cloves of Garlic, Minced
- ½ Cup of Onion, Minced
- ¾ Pound of Beef, Lean and Ground
- 1 Pound of Italian Style Sausage, Sweet Variety
- ½ Cup of Water, Warm
- 12 Ounces of Tomato Sauce
- 12 Ounces of Tomato Paste
- 28 Ounces of Tomatoes, Crushed
- ¼ teaspoons of Black Pepper, For Taste
- ½ teaspoons of Fennel, Seeds Only
- 1 teaspoon of Italian Seasoning
- 1 ½ teaspoons of Basil, Dried
- 1 tablespoon of Salt for Taste
- 2 Tablespoons of Sugar
- 2 Tablespoons of Parsley, Fresh and Finely Chopped

Ingredients for Cheese Filling:

- ½ teaspoons of Salt
- 2 Tablespoons of Parsley, Fresh and Finely Chopped
- 1 Egg, Whole and Slightly Beaten
- 16 Ounces of Ricotta Cheese

sssssssssssssssssssssssssssssssssssssssssss

Procedure:

1. Preheat your oven to 400 degrees.

2. While your oven is heating up the first thing that you will want to do is brown your ground beef and Italian sausage. Once browned add in your onions and garlic and continue cooking for an additional 5 minutes or until the onions are translucent and the garlic is fragrant.

3. Then add in your remaining meat sauce ingredients, making sure that you stir everything well to combine it together. Cover your pan and let your sauce simmer for at least 1 hour. After this time remove from heat and set aside, making sure that you stir it every now and again.

4. Then use a spate large sized pot and bring about 6 to 8 cups of water to a boil. Once boiling add in your lasagna sheets and allow to cook for at least 10 minutes or until tender. Once cooked drain your pasta and rinse your noodles under running cold water. Set aside.

5. Using a large sized bowl, stir all of your ingredients for your cheese filling together until completely combined. Set aside.

6. Next pour at least 1 ½ cups of your prepared meat sauce into a large sized lasagna dish. Add a layer of pasta over the sauce and top with some of your cheese filling. Add some of your Mozzarella and Parmesan cheese. Repeat these layers until all of your ingredients have been used. Finish with a thick layer of both your cheeses.

7. Cover your baking dish with some aluminum foil and place into your oven to bake for at least 25 minutes.

8. After this time remove your lasagna and removed the aluminum foil. Place back into your oven to continue baking for an additional 25 minutes. Remove and allow to cool for at least 10 minutes before servings.

3) Homemade Italian Style Beef

This beef recipe is a great dish to make if you want to enjoy an Italian style sandwich or whether you want to serve this alongside a bed of pasta. The meat is incredibly savory and very succulent, making it one dish that you won't want to stop making.

Yield: 3 Pounds of Shredded Beef Chuck Roast

Cooking Time: 7 Hours

List of Ingredients:

- ¼ Cup of Italian Dressing, Dry
- 3 Pounds of Beef Chuck Roast
- 1 Cup of Water
- 2 Cups of Pepperoncini Peppers, Jarred

ssssssssssssssssssssssssssssssssssssssssssss

Procedure:

1. The first thing that you will want to do is rub your dry Italian dressing mix over your roast. Then place your roast into a slow cooker.

2. Pour your water over your roast and cover. Set to cook on the highest setting and allow to cook for the next 6 hours.

3. After this time remove the cover of the slow cooker and use two forks to shred your meat.

4. Stir in your peppers along with their juices and cover the slow cooker again. Continue to cook for another hour.

5. After this time turn off your slow cooker and serve your meat on sandwich rolls or alongside a side of pasta. Enjoy!

4) Italian Style Stuffed Peppers

Stuffed Peppers make for an excellent appetizer dish that will satisfy your entire family. They are mouthwatering delicious and will satisfy all of your taste buds.

Yield: 4 Stuffed Peppers

Cooking Time: 35 Minutes

List of Ingredients:

- 4 Peppers, Red, Green and Yellow Variety, Tops Cut and Seeds Removed
- 1 Pound of Italian Sausage, Hot Variety and Cut into Small Pieces
- ½ Cup of Onions, Large In Size and Finely Chopped
- 2 Cloves of Garlic, Minced
- 1 Can of Tomatoes, Finely Diced
- 2 teaspoons of Italian Seasoning
- 1 Cup of Rice, Fully Cooked
- Some Olive Oil
- Dash of Salt and Pepper for Taste
- 1 Cup of Mozzarella Cheese, Finely Shredded
- Some Basil for Garnish, Fresh

sssssssssssssssssssssssssssssssssssssssssss

Procedure:

1. The first thing that you will want to do is cook up your sausage and onions in a bit of olive oil until the sausage are completely browned. Then add in your garlic and cook for an additional 3 minutes.

2. Next mix in your diced tomatoes and Italian seasoning. Continue cooking your mixture over low heat for the next 5 minutes.

3. Then mix in your rice. Season with a dash of salt and pepper to your taste and stir to completely combine.

4. Next place your cooked sausage mixture into your hollowed out peppers and place them onto a generously greased baking pan. Top off with your mozzarella cheese and garnish with a bit of fresh basil.

5. Place into your oven and bake at 350 degrees for at least 25 minutes or until your peppers are nice and tender. Remove and cool before serving. Enjoy!

5) Easy Salmon in Foil

It is no secret that seafood is one of the hallmarks of great Italian cuisine. Well, with this recipe you can enjoy a tasty and filling seafood dinner without all of the hassle.

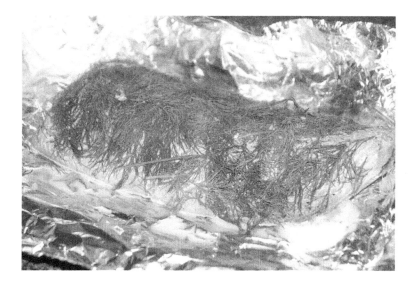

Yield: 4 Salmon Fillets

Cooking Time: 35 Minutes

List of Ingredients:

- 4 Fillets of Salmon, Wild Caught Variety
- 2 teaspoons Plus 2 Tablespoons of Olive Oil
- 1 teaspoon of Oregano, Dried
- 1 teaspoon of Thyme, Dried
- 2 Tablespoons of Lemon Juice, Fresh
- 2 Shallots, Finely Chopped
- 1 ¾ Cups of Tomatoes, Finely Chopped
- Dash of Salt and Pepper for Taste

sssssssssssssssssssssssssssssssssssssssssss

Procedure:

1. The first thing that you will want to do is preheat your oven to 400 degrees.

2. While your oven is heating up season your salmon fillets with a dash of salt and pepper. Then drizzle at least 2 teaspoons of your olive oil over the fillets.

3. Next using a medium sized bowl stir together all of your remaining ingredients until thoroughly combined. Set this mixture aside.

4. Next cut out at least 4 pieces of aluminum foil, making sure that they are large enough to wrap your salmon fillets in them. Once you have your sheet wrap each of your salmon fillets in each piece of aluminum foil, making sure that the oil side are face down.

5. Roll up the foil so that the fillets are almost incased on all sides. Before your close up the salmon spoon in your prepared mixture over the salmon and roll the ends together, sealing the salmon inside.

6. Place your salmon packets onto a baking sheet and place into your oven to bake for the next 25 minutes. After this time remove your packets and open them carefully, making sure that you are wary of the releasing steam. Allow to cool slightly and serve right away. Enjoy!

6) Easy Italian Style Potato Salad

If you are looking for another great appetizer recipe to compliment any of your Italian dishes, this is the perfect recipe for you. It is easy to make and is one potato salad dish that you are going to want to make over and over again.

Yield: 4 Servings

Cooking Time: 1 Hour and 40 Minutes

List of Ingredients:

- 4 Cloves of Garlic, Crushed
- 14 Cup of Parsley, Finely Chopped
- 1 Pound of Potatoes, Red Variety
- ¼ Cup of Olive Oil
- Dash of Salt and Pepper for Taste

ssssssssssssssssssssssssssssssssssssssssss

Procedure:

1. With the skin of your potatoes still attached, boil your potatoes in some water until they are nice and tender.

2. While your potatoes are boiling, crush up your garlic in a small sized bowl. Then add in your chopped up parsley and olive oil. Stir well until evenly combined.

3. Once your potatoes are fully cooked and still hot, chop up your potatoes in to small pieces and add to your garlic mix. Toss your potatoes roughly until thoroughly coated in your mixture. Then season with a dash of salt and pepper for your particular taste.

4. Allow you potatoes to sit for at least an hour before serving. Enjoy!

7) Sweet Tasting Lemon Ricotta Cookies

If you are looking for an easy snack recipe to create and that will end off your dinner in a very good way, then this is the recipe for you. These cookies are so tasty I guarantee that your entire family won't be able to get enough of them.

Yield: 24 Cookies

Cooking Time: 40 Minutes

Ingredients for the Cookies:

- 1 teaspoon of Salt
- 1 teaspoon of Baking Powder
- 2 ½ Cups of Flour, All Purpose
- 2 Cups of Sugar
- 1 Stick of Butter, Unsalted and Softened
- 2 Eggs, Whole
- 1 Lemon, Zest Only
- 3 Tablespoons of Lemon Juice
- 1 ¾ Cup of Ricotta Cheese

Ingredients for Your Lemon Glaze:

- 1 Lemon, Zested
- 3 Tablespoons of Lemon Juice, Fresh
- 1 ½ Cups of Confectioner's Sugar

sssssssssssssssssssssssssssssssssssssssssss

Procedure:

1. The first thing that you will want to do is preheat your oven to 375 degrees. While your oven is heating up use some parchment paper to line a large sized cookie sheet. Set aside for later use.

2. Then sift together your first three cookie ingredients in a medium to large sized bowl.

3. Using a separate medium to large sized bowl cream your butter and sugar together for at least 3 minutes.

4. In your butter and sugar mixture beat in one egg at a time until thoroughly mixed. Then add in your remaining cookie ingredients and stir to completely combine.

5. Add in your dry ingredients and continue mixing until you have a thick cookie batter on your hands.

6. Then scoop out at least 2 tablespoons of cookie onto your prepared cookie sheet. Continue until you use up all of your cookie dough.

7. Place your cookies into your oven to bake for at least 15 minutes. After 15 minutes remove from the oven and set to cool completely.

8. While your cookies are cooling stir together all of your glaze ingredients in a small sized bowl. Once your cookies are cooled pour at least ½ teaspoons of your glaze onto each cookie.

9. Allow your cookies to sit out for at least 2 hours to allow the glaze to harden. Serve right away or store your extra in an airtight container. Enjoy!

8) Italian Style Sausage Tortellini Soup

This is a great soup recipe to enjoy whenever you are wanting to make an easy lunch or dinner dish. It is incredibly filling, savory and absolutely delicious. I promise, this dish will please even the pickiest of eaters in your family.

Yield: 6 Servings

Cooking Time: 1 Hour

List of Ingredients:

- 1 Pound of Italian Style Sausage, Sweet and With Casings Removed
- 2 Cloves of Garlic, Crushed
- 1 Cup of Onion, Finely Chopped
- ½ teaspoons of Basil, Fresh
- ½ teaspoons of Oregano, Dried
- ½ Cup of Red Wine
- ½ Cup of Water
- 5 Cups of Beef Broth
- 1 Cup of Carrots, Finely Sliced
- 4 Tomatoes, Finely Chopped
- 8 Ounces of Tomato Sauce
- 3 Tablespoons of Parsley, Fresh and Finely Chopped
- 1 ½ Cups of Zucchini
- 1 Cup of Tortellini
- Some Parmesan Cheese for Serving

ssssssssssssssssssssssssssssssssssssssssssss

Procedure:

1. Using a large sized skillet placed over medium to high heat, brown your sausage until thoroughly browned. Once browned remove from skillet and make sure that you save at least 1 tablespoon of the sausage drippings.

2. Using the same pan sauté your garlic and onions until the onions become translucent and the garlic becomes fragrant. Return your sausage back into the skillet.

3. Add in the next eight ingredients into your skillet and stir thoroughly to combine. Increase the heat to high and allow your mixture to reach a boil.

4. Once boiling reduce the heat to a simmer and allow to simmer for at least 30 minutes.

5. After 30 minutes add in your parsley and zucchini and stir well to combine. Cover your pan and let your mixture simmer for another 20 minutes.

6. After 20 minutes add in your tortellini and cover again. Allow your soup to continue cooking for an additional 10 minutes before removing from heat.

7. Ladle your soup into soup bowl and serve with a sprinkle of parmesan cheese over each bowl. Serve while still piping hot and enjoy!

9) Hearty Chicken Tetrazzini

Here is yet another pasta recipe that I know you are going to love. It is incredibly easy to make and will leave you feeling full for the rest of the day.

Yield: 6 Servings

Cooking Time: 1 Hour

List of Ingredients:

- 9 Tablespoons of Butter, Softened
- 2 Tablespoons of Olive Oil
- 4 Chicken Breasts, Boneless and Skinned
- 2 ¼ teaspoons of Salt
- 1 ¼ teaspoons of Black Pepper
- 1 Pound of Mushrooms, White and Finely Sliced
- 5 Cloves of Garlic, Crushed
- 1 Onion, Finely Diced
- 1 tablespoon of Thyme, Fresh and Finely Chopped
- 1/3 cup of Flour, All Purpose
- ½ Cup of White Wine, Dry
- 1/8 teaspoons of Nutmeg, Ground
- 1 Cup of Chicken Broth
- 1 Cup of Whipping Cream, Softened
- 4 Cups of Milk, Whole
- 12 Ounces of Linguine
- ¼ Cup of Parsley, Fresh and Finely Chopped
- ¾ Cup of Peas, Frozen
- ¼ Cup of Bread Crumbs
- 1 Cup of Parmesan Cheese, Grated

sssssssssssssssssssssssssssssssssssssssssssssss

Procedure:

1. The first thing that you will want to do is preheat your oven to 450 degrees. While your oven is heating up brush the bottom of your baking dish with at least 1 tablespoon of butter. Set aside for later use.

2. Next place a skillet over medium to high heat. Add in at least 1 tablespoon of butter and 1 tablespoon of oil into the skillet.

3. Then season your chicken with some salt and pepper. Once your butter and oil is hot enough add in your chicken to your skillet and cook for at least 4 minutes on each side. Remove chicken once cooked and allow to cool for a few minutes before cutting up into small cubes. Set aside for later use.

4. Next add in another tablespoon of butter and tablespoon of oil back into your skillet. Add in your mushrooms and sauté for at least 2 minutes. Then add in your next three ingredients and continue sautéing for at least 8 more minutes.

5. Using another large sized skillet add in at least 3 tablespoons of butter and heat over medium heat. Once the butter is melted whisk in your flour and wine and allow to cook for at least 2 minutes. After 2 minutes add in your next 4 ingredients and season your mixture with a dash of salt and pepper. Stir to evenly combine.

6. Increase your heat to high and then cover your skillet as your bring your mixture to a boil. Once boiling remove the cover of your skillet and reduce the heat to medium.

7. Allow your mixture to simmer for at least 10 minutes. After 10 minutes remove your skillet from heat and set aside.

8. Next fill a large sized pot with some water. Season the water with a generous amount of salt. Bring the water to a rolling boil and place your linguini into it. Allow your pasta to cook for at least 10 minutes until the pasta is tender. Once cooked drain your water.

9. Toss your pasta in your prepared baking dish and add in your chicken, mushroom mix and fresh sauce. Toss thoroughly to coat your pasta. Add in your parsley and peas and toss again.

10. Stir your remaining two ingredients into a small sized bowl and toss again to cover. Dot your pasta with some butter and place your pasta into your oven to bake for at least 25 minutes. After this time remove your pasta from the oven and serve while still warm. Enjoy!

10) Savory Mushroom Bocconcini Salad

This is an easy mushroom salad that can double as an appetizer or a light lunch recipe. Easy to make and tastes as good as it looks.

Ingredients for Salad:

- 4 Mushrooms, Flat
- 2 Tomatoes, Large In Size and Oven Dried
- 8 Bocconcini Balls
- Some Lettuce for Garnish

Ingredients for Balsamic Dressing:

- ½ Cup of Balsamic Vinegar
- 1 Cup of Brown Sugar, Light and Packed
- 2 Shallots, Finely Chopped
- 2 Tablespoons of Vinegar, White
- Dash of Salt and Pepper for Taste

sssssssssssssssssssssssssssssssssssssssssssss

Procedure:

1. The first thing that you will want to do is place your mushrooms into a medium sized saucepan and fry them up in a bit of olive oil. Cook until the mushrooms are tender. Once tender transfer your mushrooms to a plate to cool.

2. Once your mushrooms are cool, place one mushroom per plate and top it off with at least half of your oven dried tomatoes and at least 2 balls of bocconcini.

3. Next place your lettuce around your plate for garnish.

4. Then combine all of your ingredients for your balsamic dressing until evenly combines. Pour your dressing generously over your mushrooms and serve whenever you are ready.

11) Classic Chicken Parmesan

If you are a fan of traditional Chicken Parmesan, then I know you are going to absolutely love this recipe. It is extremely filling and absolutely delicious, I know you are going to want to enjoy it again and again.

Yield: 4 Servings

Cooking Time: 35 Minutes

Ingredients for Your Pasta:

- Some Shredded Parmesan, As Needed
- 8 Ounces of Mozzarella, Buffalo Variety and Shredded
- 1 Pound of Spaghetti Pasta, Fully Cooked

Ingredients for Your Tomato-Olive Sauce:

- ¼ Cup of Olive Oil
- 2 Cloves of Garlic, Crushed
- 1 Onion, Finely Diced
- 2 Bay Leaves
- ½ Bunch of Basil, Fresh and Finely Shredded
- ½ Cup of Kalamata Olives, Pitted
- 7 Cups of Tomatoes, Peeled and Crushed
- ½ teaspoons of Sugar
- Dash of Salt and Pepper for Taste

Ingredients for Your Chicken Breasts:

- 4 Chicken Breasts, Boneless and Skinned
- ½ Cup of All Purpose Flour
- 1 tablespoon of Water
- 2 Eggs, Whole and Beaten
- 1 Cup of Bread Crumbs
- 3 Tablespoons of Olive Oil
- Dash of Salt and Pepper for Taste

ssssssssssssssssssssssssssssssssssssssssss

Procedure:

1. The first thing that you will want to do is make your tomato olive sauce. To do this place a medium to large sized saucepan over medium heat. Add in your olive oil and once it is hot enough sauté your first three ingredients for at least 5 minutes.

2. Then add in the next two ingredients. Stir to combine.

3. Add in your tomatoes and sugar and stir to combine again. Continue cooking for at least 15 more minutes. Feel free to season with a dash of salt and pepper according to your taste.

4. Next move on to preparing your chicken breast. To do this first preheat your oven to 450 degrees. While your oven is heating up pound your chicken breasts using a mallet until they are at least a half inch in thickness. Set aside for later use.

5. Then using a shallow dish combine your flour, salt and black pepper together. Once thoroughly combined set aside.

6. Using an identical dish combine your bread crumbs, dash of salt and dash of pepper until thoroughly mixed. Set this aside.

7. Then using a small sized bowl mix together your water and eggs. Set this aside.

8. Place a medium to large sized skillet over medium to high heat. Add some oil into it and once the oil is hot enough prepare to cook your chicken.

9. Next dredge your chicken in your flour, then dip it into your egg mixture and dredge it in your breadcrumbs. Repeat the entire process for all of your chicken pieces. Place your chicken into your oil and cook for at least 4 minutes on each side. Once fully cooked remove your chicken and place them into a baking sheet.

10. Next pour your premade sauce into your dish with your chicken and sprinkle your mozzarella and parmesan cheese over the top.

11. Place your chicken into your oven to bake for at least 15 minutes. Remove from oven and serve your chicken on top a bed of spaghetti. Serve right away.

12) Classic Caprese and Pesto Salad

This is a classic Italian recipe that I know for a fact you are going to enjoy thoroughly. It is incredibly filling and delicious, making it a perfect dish for an appetizer, lunch or even dinner.

Yield: 1 Salad

Cooking Time: 10 Minutes

Ingredients for the Salad:

- 2 Tomatoes, Large In Size
- A Pinch of Tulsi
- 1 Packet of Mozzarella, Buffalo Style
- Dash of Salt and Pepper

Ingredients for Sauce:

- A Pinch of Basil
- 1 Cup of Pine Nuts, Roasted
- 1 Cup of Parmesan Cheese, Finely Grated
- ½ Cup of Olive Oil
- ½ A Lemon, Juice Only and Fresh

Directions for Your Salad:

1. To make your salad first cut up your tomatoes into thick rounds and drizzle a bit of olive oil over them. Season them with a dash of salt and pepper.

2. Then cut up your mozzarella into small pieces.

3. Once done arrange your tomato slices with your mozzarella pieces onto a serving platter. Garnish with your tulsi and pesto sauce.

Directions for Your Pesto Sauce:

1. To make your pesto sauce combine your pine nut, fresh basil, parmesan cheese and olive oil. Thoroughly combine until you have a paste.

2. Then squeeze in your fresh lemon juice. Feel free to add in more olive oil if your paste is way too thick.

3. Drizzle your pesto sauce over your salad and serve immediately. Enjoy!

13) Classic Cippino

Here is yet another seafood dish that you are going to love. This is a great dish to serve whenever you are craving seafood or want a taste of some soul food cooking with an Italian twist.

Yield: 6 Servings

Cooking Time: 30 Minutes

List of Ingredients:

- ¾ Cup of Butter, Softened
- 1 Bunch of Parsley, Fresh and Finely Chopped
- 2 Cloves of Garlic, Crushed
- 2 Onions, Finely Diced
- 3 ½ Cups of Tomatoes, Stewed Variety
- 1 Cup of Water
- 1 ½ Cups of Wine, White Variety
- 3 ½ Cups of Chicken Broth
- ½ teaspoons of Thyme, Dried
- ½ teaspoons of Oregano, Dried
- 1 tablespoon of Basil, Dried
- 2 Bay Leaves, Fresh and Dried
- 1 ½ Cups of Crabmeat
- 1 ½ Pounds of Shrimp, Peeled and Deveined
- 1 ½ Pounds of Cod Fillet, Cut Into Cubes
- 1 ½ Pounds of Bay Scallops, Scrubbed Thoroughly
- 18 Mussels, Scrubbed and With Beards Removed
- 18 Clams, Scrubbed

ssssssssssssssssssssssssssssssssssssssssssss

Procedure:

1. The first thing that you will want to do is place a large sized saucepan over low to medium heat. Add in your butter and completely melt it. Once completely melted add in your parsley, garlic and onions to the pan and sauté them for at least 3 to 5 minutes.

2. Then cut up your tomatoes into chunks and place them into your pan. Add in your next three ingredients.

3. Add in your next four ingredients and season with a dash of salt and pepper. Stir to evenly combine and cover your pan. Allow your mixture to simmer for at least 30 minutes.

4. Then add in your remaining ingredients and bring your mixture to a rolling boil. Once boiling reduce the heat.

5. Cover and let your mixture cook while simmering for at least 7 minutes. Remove from heat and ladle into bowl. Serve with your choice of bread and enjoy.

14) Slow Cooker Style Chicken Alfredo

If you are anything like me, there will be some days where you just don't have the energy to make your favorite Italian classics. This is when your slow cooker can come in handy. This is easy Italian inspired slow cooker recipe is one that I am confident you will want to make over and over again.

Yield: 6 Servings

Cooking Time: 5 Hours and 15 Minutes

List of Ingredients:

- 2 Chicken Breasts, Boneless, Skinned and Cut into Halves
- ¼ Cup of Water
- ¼ Ounce of Italian Dressing, Dry
- 1 Clove of Garlic, Minced
- ½ Cup of Mushrooms, Canned
- 1 1/3 Cup of Cream of Chicken Soup, Condensed
- 1 Cup of Cream Cheese, Softened
- 1 Cup of Spaghetti, Freshly Cooked
- 1 tablespoon of Parsley, Fresh and Finely Chopped
- Some Non-stick Cooking Spray

ssssssssssssssssssssssssssssssssssssssssssss

Procedure:

1. First spray all sides of your slow cooker with a generous amount of cooking spray.

2. Then place your chicken into your slow cooker.

3. Using a small sized bowl stir together your water and Italian dressing until completely mixed.

4. Sprinkle your minced garlic over your chicken as well as your water and dressing mix.

5. Cover your slow cooker and set on the lowest setting. Allow your chicken to cook for at least 4 hours.

6. After this time stir in your cream of chicken soup, mushrooms and cream cheese, making sure to stir thoroughly to combine everything together.

7. Continue cooking your mixture for another hour.

8. Place your cooked spaghetti onto a place and spoon your slow cooker mixture over the top of it. Garnish with some fresh parsley and enjoy immediately.

15) Savory Alfredo Peppered Shrimp

If you are a fan of shrimp, then you need to try this recipe for yourself. Containing the perfect combination of Alfredo and shrimp, this is certainly one dish that is going to leave you drooling for more.

Yield: 2 Servings

Cooking Time: 30 Minutes

List of Ingredients:

- 1 ½ Cups of Penne Pasta
- 2 Tablespoons of Olive Oil
- ¼ Cup of Butter, Softened
- 1 Onion, Large In Size and Chopped Finely
- ½ Pound of Portobello Mushrooms, Finely Chopped
- 1 Red Bell Pepper, Finely Chopped
- 2 Cloves of Garlic, Crushed
- 1 Pound of Shrimp, Peeled and Deveined
- ½ Cup of Cream
- ½ Cup of Romano Cheese, Finely Grated
- 1 ¾ Cup of Alfredo Sauce, Your Favorite Kind
- 1 teaspoon of Cayenne Pepper
- ¼ Cup of Parsley, Fresh and Finely Chopped
- Dash of Salt and Pepper for Taste

ssssssssssssssssssssssssssssssssssssssssssss

1. The first thing that you will want to do is fill up a large sized pot with water. Season the water with a dash of salt and place over high heat. Bring the water to a boil. Once the water begins to boil add in your penne pasta and allow to cook for 10 minutes or until tender. Once cooked drain your pasta and set aside.

2. Then using a medium sized saucepan and place over medium heat. Add some oil and butter and once fully melted and hot, add in your onions. Sauté your onions for at least 2 minutes before adding in your mushrooms, bell peppers and garlic. Continue to cook for an additional 2 minutes.

3. Add in your shrimp and continue cooking until firm.

4. Then add in your cream, Alfredo sauce and Romano cheese, making sure to stir until completely combined. Sprinkle with a dash of salt, pepper and cayenne pepper. Remove mixture from heat.

5. Next combine your pasta and sauce together until thoroughly tossed and coated.

6. Last sprinkle with some parsley and serve with your choice of bread. Enjoy!

16) Classic Bruschetta

Bruschetta is a delicious appetizer recipe that can be made alongside any Italian dish that you make. It is light yet delicious, making your crave your dinner or lunch recipe even more.

Yield: 20 Minutes

Cooking Time: 4 Servings

List of Ingredients:

- 1 Loaf of Country Style Bread
- A Few Cloves of Garlic
- 2 Tomatoes, Large In Size and Finely Chopped
- A Few Basil Leaves, Fresh
- 5 Tablespoons of Olive Oil
- 4 Mushrooms, Large In Size and Finely Sliced
- 1 Glove of Onion, Finely Grated
- 1 Red Chili, Finely Chopped
- 1 tablespoon of Butter
- Dash of Salt and Pepper

Directions for Your Bread:

1. The first thing that you will want to do is cut up your country style bread into two halves.

2. Then slice up your cloves of garlic and rub onto the surface of your bread halves.

3. Drizzle some of your olive oil on top.

4. Next place your bread slices into your oven and broil for at least 5 minutes

Directions for Your Mushroom Topping:

1. Now mix together your butter, olive oil and thyme until thoroughly mixed.

2. Next add in your sliced mushrooms and chilies. Mix again until thoroughly combined. Season with a dash of salt and pepper.

3. Pour this mixture into an oil saucepan over medium heat. Cook for at least 5 to 7 minutes or until piping hot.

Directions for Your Tomato Topping:

1. To make this topping place your tomatoes, dash of salt, dash of pepper, olive oil and basil together in a small sized bowl and mix together until thoroughly combined.

2. Then place your toasted bread onto a serving platter and pile high with both of your toppings. Serve right away and enjoy!

17) Classic Zuppa Toscana

This easy stew dish is great for those cold winter nights or whenever you are craving an easy Italian style dish to enjoy.

Yield: 3 Servings

Cooking Time: 25 Minutes

List of Ingredients:

- 1 Pound of Italian Sausage, Mild In Taste
- 1 ¼ teaspoons of Red Pepper, Crushed
- 4 Strips of Bacon, Roughly Chopped
- 1 tablespoon of Garlic, Minced
- 1 Onion, Finely Chopped
- 8 ½ Cups of Chicken Broth, Homemade Preferable
- 6 Potatoes, Finely Sliced
- 1 Cup of Cream, Heavy
- ¼ Bunch of Spinach, Fresh and With the Stems Removed

sssssssssssssssssssssssssssssssssssssssssss

Procedure:

1. Using a large sized saucepan, brown your sausage evenly with some red pepper flakes. Allow to cook for at least 15 minutes or until thoroughly browned. Remove from heat and set aside.

2. Using the same pan, cook your bacon until crispy or to your liking. This should take about 10 to 20 minutes. Drain half of your bacon drippings, making sure to save the remainder.

3. Add your garlic to the bacon drippings and cook for at least 5 minutes.

4. Then add in your chicken broth and increase the heat to high. Allow your mixture to boil before adding in your potato slices. Allow to cook for at least 20 minutes.

5. Reduce the heat to a medium and add in your sausage and heavy cream. Stir well to incorporate. Continue cooking for an additional 5 minutes until piping hot and remove from heat.

6. Stir in your fresh spinach and ladle soup into soup bowls. Serve while still piping hot and enjoy!

18) Margherita Style Pizza

If you are a fan of pizza, then you are certainly going to enjoy this recipe. Feel free to become as creative as you wish with your pizza toppings. No matter what kind of toppings you use, I know you are going to love this pizza dish.

Yield: 1 Pizza

Cooking Time: 1 Hour and 20 Minutes

Ingredients for Your Pizza Dough:

- 2 Cups of Flour
- 1 Packet of Yeast, Fast Acting and Dry Variety
- 1 ¼ Cup of Water, Warm
- ¼ Cup of Olive Oil
- Dash of Salt for Taste
- Some Extra Virgin Olive Oil
- ½ teaspoons of Sugar

Ingredients for Your Pizza Sauce:

- 1 Cup of Mozzarella Cheese, Finely grated
- 1 Handful of Basil Leaves
- Some Olive Oil
- Chopped Up Peppers, Green, Red and Yellow Variety

Directions for Your Pizza Dough:

1. The first thing that you will want to do is mix up your flour with a dash of salt.

2. Next add yeast into your warm water and stir in your sugar. Mix thoroughly until the sugar and the yeast dissolve and set aside to sit for at least 6 to 8 minutes.

3. Then take a large sized mixing bowl and place your flour mixture into it. Create a well in the center of your flour and add in your yeast mixture and olive oil.

4. Mix together until your have a ball of dough on your hands.

5. Lightly flour a flat surface and knead your dough until it is no longer sticky. Knead for at least 10 minutes.

6. Place your ball of dough into your mixing bowl and drizzle with some extra virgin olive oil. Cover with some plastic wrap and place your bowl into a warm area to sit for at least 1 hour.

7. After an hour roll out your dough onto a flour surface until flat to your liking.

Directions for Your Toppings:

1. The first thing that you will want to do is preheat your oven to 450 degrees or higher if your oven will allow it.

2. Place your rolled out dough onto a generously greased pizza tray. Then place a thin layer of your peppers, olive oil and basil leaves. Top with as much mozzarella cheese as you want.

3. Place your pizza into your oven to bake for at least 12 minutes. Remove from oven and drizzle with some more extra virgin olive oil. Serve while still piping hot and enjoy.

19) Slow Cooker Style Eggplant Parmesan

Here is yet another slow cooker style recipe for you. It is easy to make and will leave you certainly craving for more.

Yield: 6 Servings

Cooking Time: 6 Hours

List of Ingredients:

- 4 Eggplants, Peeled and Finely Sliced
- 1 tablespoon of Salt
- 3 Tablespoons of Flour, All Purpose
- 1/3 Cup of Water
- 2 Eggs, Whole
- 1 Cup of Olive Oil
- ½ Cup of Parmesan Cheese, Finely Grated
- 1/3 Cup of Bread Crumbs, Seasoned
- 4 Cups of Marinara Sauce
- 2 Cups of Mozzarella Cheese, Finely Sliced

ssssssssssssssssssssssssssssssssssssssssssss

Procedure:

1. The first thing that you will want to do is season your eggplant slices with a generous amount of salt. Allow to sit out for at least 30 minutes.

2. While your eggplants are sitting out take a medium sized bowl and beat together your flour, water and eggs together until evenly mixed. Set this mixture aside.

3. Next set a medium to large sized skillet over medium heat. Pour your oil into it. Once the oil is hot enough dredge your eggplant slices into your floured mixture and then into your oil. Dry your eggplant slices until they are golden brown in color. Continue to repeat until you have used up all of your eggplant. Set aside to cool.

4. Then using a separate, stir together your parmesan and bread crumbs until thoroughly mixed.

5. Next line the bottom of your slow cooker with at least one quarter of your fried eggplant. Then follow up by spreading a quarter of your parmesan mixture over the eggplant followed by a quarter of your marinara sauce. Last cover that with a quarter of your mozzarella. Continue that process until all of your ingredients have been used up.

6. Cover your slow cooker and set to the lowest setting. Allow your mixture to cook for at least 5 hours. After this time slice up your eggplant, garnish and serve right away.

20) Spaghetti Marinara

If you are looking for an easy pasta recipe to make that tastes delicious and will leave your feeling full for the rest of the day, then this is the perfect recipe for you. It is a classic Italian dish that your entire family will love.

Yield: 6 to 8 Servings

Cooking Time: 2 Hours and 15 Minutes

List of Ingredients:

- 1 Pound of Spaghetti
- 1 Can of Tomatoes, Pureed and Plum Variety
- 1 Can of Tomato Paste
- ½ Cup of Wine, Dry Red Variety
- 1 Onion, Finely Chopped
- 1 teaspoon of Basil, Dried
- 1 teaspoon of Oregano, Dried
- 4 Cloves of Garlic, Crushed
- ¼ Cup of Parsley, Fresh and Roughly Chopped
- 2 Tablespoons of Olive Oil
- Some Parmesan Cheese, Finely Grated

sssssssssssssssssssssssssssssssssssssssssss

Procedure:

1. The first thing that you will want to do is cook up your onions and garlic in a medium sized sauté pan set over medium to high heat for at least 10 minutes. Then add in your tomato puree, tomato paste and dry wine. Mix until thoroughly combined.

2. Next add in your basil and oregano and cover. Cook your sauce over low heat for the next 2 hours. Then add in your fresh parsley. Continue cooking for the next 5 minutes.

3. While your sauce is cooking, cook your pasta in a generous amount of water for at least 10 minutes or until the pasta is al dente.

4. Once the pasta is done place onto a large sized serving platter and top off with your prepared marinara sauce. Sprinkle with a generous amount of Parmesan cheese and serve whenever you are ready. Enjoy!

21) Easy Italian Style Penne and Pasta

This is yet another pasta recipe that I know you are going to love. It is easy to make and smothered in cheese, making it one of the best tasting Italian dishes in this entire cookbook.

Yield: 4 Servings

Cooking Time: 30 Minutes

List of Ingredients:

- 1 Pound of Beef, Ground
- 4 Cups of Penne Pasta
- 3 ½ Cups of Spaghetti Sauce, Your Favorite Kind
- ¾ Cup of Parmesan Cheese, Finely Grated
- 3 Cups of Colby Jack Cheese, Shredded

sssssssssssssssssssssssssssssssssssssssssss

Procedure:

1. The first thing that you will want to do is cook up your penne pasta in some boiling water until tender. Remove and drain. Set aside.

2. Using a medium sized skillet, brown your ground beef. Once browned drain your beef and mix together with your penne pasta.

3. Mix together your beef, pasta, spaghetti sauce and parmesan cheese together until completely mixed.

4. Place this mixture into a large sized baking dish and top off with your remaining Parmesan cheese and Colby Jack Cheese.

5. Place into your oven to bake at 350 degrees for at least 20 minutes. After this time remove from oven and allow to cool slightly before serving. Enjoy!

22) Traditional Mushroom Risotto

This is yet another traditional Italian dish that your entire family will drool over. It is savory and filling, making it the perfect dinner dish to prepare.

Yield: 4 Servings

Cooking Time: 45 Minutes

List of Ingredients:

- 1 tablespoon of Olive Oil
- 1 Onion, Medium in Size and Finely Chopped
- ¼ Cup of Butter, Melted
- 1 Cup of Mushrooms, Finely Sliced
- ½ Cup of Arborio Rice
- ¼ Cup of White Wine, Your Favorite Kind
- 4 Cups of Chicken Stock, Hot
- 1/3 Cup of Parmesan Cheese, Finely Grated
- 1 tablespoon of Parsley, Fresh and Chopped
- ¼ Cup of Butter, Melted and Extra
- Dash of Salt and Pepper for Taste

sssssssssssssssssssssssssssssssssssssssssss

Procedure:

1. The first thing that you will want to do is cook up your onions and mushrooms together in some oil and butter until soft and golden in color.

2. Then add in your rice and cook until pellucid.

3. Ladle in 1 cup of your chicken stock and stir to mix well. Cover and cook for an additional 5 minutes until your rice is completely dry.

4. Add in the rest of your chicken stock, stir again and cover. Continue cooking your rice mixture for at least 25 minutes. Season with a dash of salt and pepper.

5. Remove from heat and stir in your parmesan cheese, fresh parsley and some more salt and pepper if you desire. Mix and serve right away. Enjoy.

23) Italian Style Meatloaf

If you are a fan of meatloaf, then you are going to love this recipe. It is easy to make and makes a lot of it, making it the perfect recipe to feed a large number of people.

Yield: 1 Meatloaf

Cooking Time: 1 Hour and 15 Minutes

List of Ingredients:

- 2 teaspoons of Canola Oil
- ½ Onion, Finely Diced
- 2 Bell Peppers, Finely Diced
- 3 Mushrooms, Button Variety and Finely Chopped
- 3 Cloves of Garlic, Finely Chopped
- 1 Pound of Ground Beef, Lean
- ¾ Cup of Breadcrumbs, Italian Seasoned Variety
- ½ Cup of Parmesan Cheese
- 2 Eggs, Large In Size and Slightly Beaten
- 3 Tablespoons of Basil, Fresh and Finely Chopped
- ½ teaspoons of Oregano, Dried
- 3 teaspoons of Worcestershire Sauce
- 3 teaspoons of Balsamic Vinegar
- Dash of Salt and Pepper for Taste
- 1 Cup of Marinara Sauce

sssssssssssssssssssssssssssssssssssssssssssss

Procedure:

1. The first thing that you will want to do is preheat your oven to 350 degrees. While your oven is heating up grease up a baking dish with a generous amount of cooking spray.

2. Next heat up a large sized skillet over medium heat with some olive oil. Once the oil is hot enough add in your onions, pepper and mushrooms. Cook for at least 5 minutes until completely tender. Once tender add in your garlic and cook over low heat for at least a minute. Remove from heat and set aside to cool completely.

3. Then mix together your ground beef with your breadcrumbs, basil, oregano, balsamic vinegar, parmesan cheese, eggs and Worcestershire sauce. Mix with your onion mixture and season with a generous amount of salt and pepper. Using your hands combine everything together until well mixed.

4. Place this mixture into your greased baking dish and top off with your marinara sauce poured over the top.

5. Place your pan into the oven to bake for at least 1 hour or until your meat is completely tender. After this time remove from oven and allow it to sit for at least 10 minutes. Serve.

24) Baked Spaghetti and Meatballs

This is a healthier take on the traditional spaghetti and meatball recipe that you may have loved as a child. This dish is incredibly easy to make and will surely please even the pickiest of eaters. This makes a lot of spaghetti so this is an ideal dish to make if you plan of feeding a large group of people.

Yield: 8 Servings

Cooking Time: 1 Hour and 20 Minutes

Ingredients for Your Meatballs:

- 1 Pound of Beef, Ground
- 1 Pound of Pork, Ground
- 2 Eggs, Large In Size and Slightly Beaten
- 2 Eggs, Large In Size and Beaten Slightly
- ½ Cup of Parmesan Cheese, Finely Grated
- 1/3 Cup of Breadcrumbs, Italian Style
- 2 Tablespoons of Garlic, Finely Chopped
- 1 teaspoon of Salt
- 1 teaspoon of Black Pepper, Fresh and Ground
- 1/3 Cup of Milk, Whole
- ½ teaspoons of Oregano, Dried
- 2 Tablespoons of Parsley, Dried and Roughly Chopped

Ingredients for Your Spaghetti:

- 1 Package of Spaghetti
- 3 Tablespoons of Oil
- 3 Cup of Mozzarella Cheese, Finely Shredded
- 1 Cup of Parmesan Cheese, Finely Grated
- 3 Eggs, Large In Size and Slightly Beaten
- 1 teaspoon of Salt
- Dash of Black Pepper
- 2 Jars of Spaghetti Sauce, Your Favorite Kind
- Some Parmesan Cheese, Finely Grated

Directions for Your Meatballs:

1. The first thing that you will want to do is combine all of your ingredients together in a large sized mixing bowl.

2. Then shape your meat into small sized balls and place onto a lightly greased baking tray. Place your meatballs into your oven to bake at 350 degrees for at least 25 minutes or until thoroughly cooked.

Directions for Your Pasta:

1. Next you will need to cook up your spaghetti in a pot of boiling water for at least 10 minutes or until tender. Drain your pasta.

2. Next mix together your spaghetti with at least 3 Tablespoons of your olive oil and let it cool slightly.

3. Mix in your beaten eggs, mozzarella cheese, parmesan cheese and dash of salt and pepper. Use your hands to toss roughly until thoroughly coated.

4. Place your cooked spaghetti into a shallow baking dish and cover with your baked meatballs.

5. Top of your dish with your pasta sauce until all used up. Cover with some aluminum foil and bake at 350 degrees for about 45 minutes or until bubbly.

6. Remove from oven and cover with some more mozzarella cheese. Place back into your oven to bake for at least 5 minutes or until the cheese has completely melted. Remove from oven and serve once slightly cooled. Enjoy!

25) Classic Italian Potato Salad

Here is yet another easy "salad" recipe for you to enjoy. This potato salad recipe is great for small picnics or to bring with you to a large family gathering. I guarantee everybody you know will be begging for this delicious recipe.

Yield: 4 Servings

Cooking Time: 35 Minutes

List of Ingredients:

- 2 Pounds of Potatoes, Peeled and Cut Into Small Pieces
- ¾ Cup of Italian Dressing, Your Favorite Brand
- 2 Tablespoons of Mayonnaise
- 2 Tablespoons of Parsley Leaves, Fresh and Coarsely Chopped
- 1 Red Bell Pepper, Small in Size and Finely Chopped
- 2 Tablespoons of Olive, Pitted, Ripe and Finely Sliced
- Some Black Pepper for Taste

sssssssssssssssssssssssssssssssssssssssssss

Procedure:

1. The first thing that you will want to do is spread your potatoes into a large size pot filled with water. Season the water with a dash of salt if you desire. Once the water is boiling reduce the heat to a simmer and allow your potatoes to cook uncovered until they are tender. This should take about 8 minutes. Drain and set aside.

2. Next combine your Italian dressing, mayo and parsley together in a small sized bowl and combine until evenly mixed.

3. Add in your red peppers and olives and stir again to combine.

4. Add this mix to your chopped up cooked potatoes and toss roughly with your hands until evenly coated. Allow to cool down in room temperature and serve whenever you are ready. Enjoy!

26) Italian Style Wine Biscuits

These biscuits make for a tasty snack or a pleasing appetizer dish for you to enjoy. Easy to make and incredibly filling, this dish is certainly a dish that you are going to want to make over and over again.

Yield: 4 Servings

Cooking Time: 50 Minutes

List of Ingredients:

- 2 ½ Cup of Flour
- 2 Tablespoons of Black Pepper, Ground and Coarse
- 6 Tablespoons of Sugar, White
- 1 tablespoon of Salt
- 2 Tablespoons of Baking Powder
- ½ Cup of Wine, Dry and Red Variety
- ¼ Cup of Vegetable Oil

ssssssssssssssssssssssssssssssssssssssssssss

Procedure:

1. The first thing that you will want to do is mix together your flour, salt, pepper, sugar and baking powder in a medium sized mixing bowl until thoroughly mixed.

2. Next mix your wine and vegetable oil together in a separate small sized bowl until evenly mixed.

3. Then combine your dry ingredients and wet ingredients together for at least one minute or until smooth in consistency. Then cover your bowl with some plastic wrap and place into your refrigerator to chill for at least 1 hour.

4. After an hour break up your dough into bite sized piece about the size of a walnut. Form your dough into small sized bagel shaped pieces. Place your completely dough rings onto a lightly greased baking sheet.

5. Put your baking sheet into your oven to bake at 375 degrees for at least 35 to 40 minutes or until golden brown in color. Remove from oven and allow to cool completely. Serve whenever you are ready.

About the Author

Allie Allen developed her passion for the culinary arts at the tender age of five when she would help her mother cook for their large family of 8. Even back then, her family knew this would be more than a hobby for the young Allie and when she graduated from high school, she applied to cooking school in London. It had always been a dream of the young chef to study with some of Europe's best and she made it happen by attending the Chef Academy of London.

After graduation, Allie decided to bring her skills back to North America and open up her own restaurant. After 10 successful years as head chef and owner, she decided to sell her business and pursue other career avenues. This monumental decision led Allie to her true calling, teaching. She also started to write e-books for her students to study at home for practice. She is now the proud author of several e-books and gives private and semi-private cooking lessons to a range of students at all levels of experience.

Stay tuned for more from this dynamic chef and teacher when she releases more informative e-books on cooking and baking in the near future. Her work is infused with stores and anecdotes you will love!

Author's Afterthoughts

I can't tell you how grateful I am that you decided to read my book. My most heartfelt thanks that you took time out of your life to choose my work and I hope you find benefit within these pages.

There are so many books available today that offer similar content so that makes it even more humbling that you decided to buying mine.

Tell me what you thought! I am eager to hear your opinion and ideas on what you read as are others who are looking for a good book to buy. Leave a review on Amazon.com so others can benefit from your wisdom!

With much thanks,

Allie Allen

Made in the USA
Monee, IL
11 December 2020